THREE WORDS

DON'T EVER Q

RALPH BROOKS

THREE WORDS
Don't Ever Quit

iUniverse books may be ordered through booksellers or by contacting:

iUniverse
1663 Liberty Drive
Bloomington, IN 47403
www.iuniverse.com
1-800-Authors (1-800-288-4677)

ISBN: 978-1-5320-6892-8 (sc)
ISBN: 978-1-5320-6894-2 (hc)
ISBN: 978-1-5320-6893-5 (e)

Library of Congress Control Number: 2019903563

Print information available on the last page.

iUniverse rev. date: 04/17/2019

TRES PALABRAS
No renuncies nunca

Copyright © 2019 Ralph Brooks

Puede hacer pedidos de libros de iUniverse en librerías o poniéndose en contacto con:

iUniverse
1663 Liberty Drive
Bloomington, IN 47403
www.iuniverse.com
1-800-Authors (1-800-288-4677)

ISBN: 978-1-5320-6892-8 (tapa blanda)
ISBN: 978-1-5320-6894-2 (tapa dura)
ISBN: 978-1-5320-6893-5 (libro electrónico)

Número de Control de la Biblioteca del Congreso: 2019903563

Información sobre impresión disponible en la última página.

Fecha de revisión de iUniverse: 03/29/2019

Contents

Contenidos

ALABAMA MADE ME
FLORIDA RAISED ME
PHILIPPINES CHANGED ME

ABOUT THE BOOK

Children's books are fascinating and leave us with great memories. The most important things in life are not what you can see, but what you can read and forever feel in your heart.

Special Bonus

Ralph V. Brooks

Introduction

In 2009, I gained the opportunity to travel to Manila, Philippines with my friend, Tomas Cintron. Little did I know I would fall in love with the entire country. Filipinos are among some of the nicest people in the world. The people along with their culture reminded me of my upbringing in Eufaula, Alabama. While there I visited Cebu, San Fernando, Cavite, Baguio, Davao, Batangas, Angeles City, Pandacan, Mariveles, Corregidor Island, Pilar (Mount Samat) and Subic Bay. Paco, Manila is the place that I have my best memories.

This is where I met the Marinduque family. They showed so much respect and gave me so much love that I continued to visit them for the next 9 years. I am the proud godfather to their daughters, Ana-Marie, and a new baby girl Helena. I was honored and happy to receive the kind gesture, and I kindly accepted. Their dad, Diomar (Barangay Official) would cook throughout the week chicken tinola soup, fried bangus, and panic. They are my favorite Filipino foods. He told me one day while cutting me some mango in the kitchen that I was welcome in his home anytime that I came to the Philippines. I still long for the taste of his food as his style of cooking is irreplaceable. He passed away on December 31, 2018. My heart will forever be in pain of missing him. His wife, Virginia calls me her son and every time I would leave to come back to the United States. We both would cry. She would tell me that she loves me and could never forget me. They made me see that you can have so little but so much when you pull together as a family.

I had 500 peso in my pocket and felt like the richest man in the world in the Philippines. It is one thing I did know, I could go to Jollibee's at Harrison Plaza on the corner of Pablo Ocampo Street. I could get me a 2-piece burger steak with mushrooms, rice and gravy, and a regular soft drink for less than 100 peso and have a great meal. Then, I would take a Jeepney to go to Pandacan and play basketball with the kid's in the neighborhood. You can't put a price on a true peace of mind. Those are memories that will last with me for a lifetime.

Dedication Page

My gift to Manny Pacquiao is honoring him on my Children's book; no fighter in history has won world titles in more weight classes than Manny Pacquiao. The Filipino legend from Kibawe, Bukidnon province, Mindanao, Philippines (Home of the Champ) has won titles in eight divisions as shown below.

1. Flyweight Title: December 4, 1998 in Phuttamonthon, Thailand

2. Junior Featherweight Title: June 23, 2001, in his first fight in the United States at the MGM Grand Arena in Las Vegas.

3. Featherweight Title: November 15, 2003 at Alamodome, San Antonio, Texas, United States.

4. Junior Lightweight Title: March 15, 2008 in Las Vegas, Nevada, United States.

5. Lightweight Title: June 28, 2008 in Las Vegas, Nevada, United States.

6. Junior Welterweight Title: May 2, 2009 in Las Vegas, Nevada, United States.

7. Welterweight Title: November 14, 2009 in Las Vegas, Nevada, United States.

8. Junior Middleweight Title: November 13, 2010 at Cowboys Stadium, Arlington, Texas, United States.

I remember walking into the ring in San Antonio, Texas and getting booed by everyone. I think I had one fan, my trainer Freddie Roach. I had no idea what I had done to these people. When I was in the ring fighting, instead of hearing boos, I heard nothing.

-Manny Pacquiao, Filipino Boxer and "Fighter of the Decade" for the 2000s by the Boxing Writers Association of America.

Acknowledgement

I wanted to acknowledge several individuals that have been key in assisting me through this process of publishing. Denise Benefiel, my Publishing Consultant, helped in recommending a color publishing package that fit my needs and what made sense for my book and answering my questions. Gil Maley, my Check IN Coordinator, provided tips while assisting me with looking for images for front and back cover of the book before submission process. Reed Samuel, Publishing Services Associate, for bridging and facilitating the cover and interior design. Martin Bower, Marketing Consultant, thank you for working with me to get my book visibility and international exposure in London, UK, Beijing, China, Frankfurt, Germany, and Guadalajara, Mexico. Patrick Jackson, Book Mentor, thank you for your advice and support with additional proofreading of the book. The instructions and suggestions provided by Denise, Gil, Reed, Martin, and Patrick made all difference and far exceeded my expectations. They all have been instrumental in making this a wonderful experience.

My thanks also go to my best friend, Darrell Ingram, Vice President of Brooks and Books. We have been friends for 14 years now. He traveled with me to the Philippines for seven years straight working on this project. He is able to share the same memories of our friends in the Philippines.

In addition, a special thank you goes to my senior editor, Sarjoo Devani. He has been the guiding force behind the edification of the poems in this book. I am eternally grateful for his support.

Sarjoo@crazedandrephrased.global

WWW.crazedandrephrased.global

BROOKS-N-BOOKS

Additional books by Ralph V. Brooks:

The Road to Number One

Ralph Brooks gives the reader a glimpse into his formative high school years. This book provides a narrative of the importance of football and the life lessons learned in the cities of Dadeville, Jackson Gap, and his hometown, Eufaula, Alabama.

Day by Day Living with Epilepsy

This is an intimate introspective of the author, Ralph Brooks, life experiences with Epilepsy. With a desire to educate the general public about this medical condition,

he provides information on the care, treatment, safety precautions and difficult decisions that face those with the condition.

Otros libros por Ralph V. Brooks:

El Camino a Ser el Número Uno

Ralph Brooks da al lector un vistazo a sus años formativos en la preparatoria. Este libro da una narrativa sobre la importancia del fútbol y sobre las lecciones de vida que obtuvo en las ciudades de Dadeville, Jackson Gap, y su ciudad local, Eufaula, Alabama.

Día a Día Viviendo con Epilepsia

Esta es una introspección íntima de las experiencias derivadas de vivir con epilepsia del autor, Ralph Brooks. Con el deseo de educar al público en general sobre esta afección médica, él provee información sobre el cuidado, tratamiento, precauciones de seguridad y las difíciles decisiones a las que aquellos con la afección se enfrentan.

The moment where you doubt whether you can fly, you cease forever being able to do it.
-Peter Pan

El momento en el que dudas si puedes volar, dejas de poder hacerlo por siempre.
-Peter Pan

Author Notes

Brooks has fond memories of reading his first Japanese haiku poem in the fourth grade. He features a collection of timeless, beautiful, fun, and rhyming classical poems for kids. Brooks' poems help children understand themselves and real life experiences. It's a thoughtful way for kids to develop a passion for reading in a musical way.

Notas del Autor

Brooks tiene gratos recuerdos de cuando leyó su primer poema haiku japonés en el cuarto grado. Él presenta una colección de poemas infantiles clásicos, eternos, bellos, divertidos y con rimas. Los poemas de Brooks ayudan a los niños a identificarse a sí mismos y a experiencias de la vida real. Es una manera considerada de que los niños desarrollen una pasión por la lectura de manera musical.

Brook's 5 Reasons for Creating the Activity Page

1. **Parents reading together with their children helps create a bond.**

I was working three jobs and had a very busy work schedule. I would read to my boys at night and it was a great way for us to bond after dad had a long day at work. There was nothing better than cuddling up with them and reading a poem or a bedtime story together. Now they write their own poems and tell their own stories!

2. **Reading develops a child's vision, creativity, and imagination.**

I would ask my boys, what they wanted to be in life. They would say dad, this is what I am going to be. The beauty would be seeing the excitement in their eyes when they would tell me what they wanted to become. This exercise is a way to encourage kids to dream, think, and do their best in reading to be able to do the things they want to do in the future. When we are engaged in a story, we are also imagining how the character feels. We use our own experiences to imagine how we feel in the same situation.

3. **Reading improves language and vocabulary skills.**

My father had a third grade level of education. He was not able to sit down and read a book to me. I did not want the same thing to for my boys. I read to my boys, different of books on different topics. I wanted them exposed to a wide range of information. Also not to limit their vocabulary skills. Different books are needed to help children about important things in life such as diversity, sharing, treating people the way you want to be treated, sharing, and being respectful to your elders. Reading together with your kids can create a thirst for knowledge. This is why my poetry book was written with a variety of different topics.

4. **Kids who read often and widely get better at it.**

My fourth grade teacher helped me build up my confidence by teaching me the importance of reading. Reading to your child leads to questions about the book and the information within. Every day after school I looked forward to meeting with my fourth grade teacher to learn more new words. I do not think there is anything better than seeing a child who loves to read to learn more about life. The more reading children do along with activities, the more quickly they will develop as readers. My football coach would always tell me practice makes perfect and reading is no different from anything else.

5. **Children's who read early do better at school.**

My boys, Patrick Brooks (21), and Brandon Brooks (18) are both great readers. They both finished high school with honors and earned football scholarships to go to college. Words cannot express my love and gratitude towards my boys and their input on this book. I started reading to them when they were six years old. I was so determined for my boys not to be behind in school the way I was in fourth grade. I wanted to pay it forward as my teacher had done for me. Every parent should focus on reading to their child early in life to avoid illiteracy.

"Children are made readers on the laps of their parents"
-Emilie Buchwald

Las 5 Razones de Brooks para Crear la Página de Actividades

1. **Que los padres lean junto a sus hijos ayuda a crear un lazo.**

Yo tenía tres trabajos y un horario laboral muy cargado. Les leía a mis hijos en la noche y esta era una buena forma de unirnos después de que papá tuviera un día largo en el trabajo. No había nada mejor que abrazarlos y leer un poema o un cuento para dormir juntos. ¡Ahora ellos escriben sus propios poemas y sus propios cuentos!

2. **La lectura desarrolla la visión, creatividad e imaginación del niño.**

Les preguntaba a mis hijos qué querían ser en su vida. Me decían "papá, esto es lo que seré." Lo bello era ver la emoción en sus ojos cuando me decían lo que querían ser. Este ejercicio es una forma de alentar a los niños a soñar, pensar y hacer lo mejor que puedan al leer para poder hacer las cosas que quieren hacer en el futuro. Cuando estamos involucrados en una historia, también nos imaginamos cómo se sienten los personajes. Usamos nuestras propias experiencias para imaginar cómo nos sentiríamos en la misma situación

3. **La lectura mejora las habilidades del lenguaje y el vocabulario.**

El nivel educativo de mi padre era del tercer grado. Él no podía sentarse a leer un libro conmigo. Yo no quería lo mismo para mis hijos. Yo le leía a mis hijos diferentes libros con temáticas distintas. Quería exponerles a un amplio espectro de información. También para no limitar sus habilidades de vocabulario. Se necesitan diversos libros para ayudarles a los niños a entender cosas importantes en la vida como la diversidad, el compartir, tratar a la gente tal como quisieras que te traten y ser respetuoso con tus mayores. Leer junto a tus hijos puede crear sed por conocimiento. Esta es la razón por la que mi libro de poesía fue escrito sobre temas diversos.

4. **Los niños que leen generalmente se vuelven mejores en ello.**

Mi maestro en el cuarto grado me ayudó a fortalecer mi confianza enseñándome la importancia de la lectura. Leerles a tus hijos les lleva preguntarse sobre el libro y a la información en este. Cada día después de la escuela yo esperaba para reunirme con mi maestro del cuarto grado para aprender más palabras nuevas. No creo que haya algo mejor que ver a un niño que ama la lectura empezar a aprender más sobre la vida. Cuanto más lean los niños, junto a otras actividades, más rápidamente se desarrollan como lectores. Mi entrenador de fútbol americano siempre me decía que la práctica hace al maestro, y la lectura no es la excepción.

5. **A los niños que leen les va mejor en la escuela.**

Mis hijos, Patrick Brooks (21) y Brandon Brooks (18) son grandes lectores. Ambos terminaron la preparatoria con honores y recibieron becas de fútbol americano para ir a la universidad. Las palabras no pueden explicar mi amor y gratitud hacia mis hijos y su aporte a este libro. Empecé a leerles cuando tenían seis años. Estaba tan determinado a que mis hijos no se atrasaran en la escuela como yo estaba en el cuarto grado. Quería devolver el favor que mi maestro de cuarto grado me había hecho. Cada padre debería centrarse en leerles a sus hijos temprano en sus vidas para evitar la incultura.

"Los niños se vuelven lectores en el regazo de sus padres"
Emilie Buchwald

My Talk To My Son

On August 7, 1997 my son cried out loud,
Seeing you come into this world, made me feel proud. There was never a doubt or a maybe,
I knew you were my baby.
When I first saw your smile,
I was so glad that you were my child.
Before you came into my life, I would sit and ponder, Of how life makes you wonder.
If life is worth living,
When all you seem to do is to be giving.
Half the time, in my mind, I felt like I was losing, Because everything was so confusing.
Just when I had put everything aside,
You came along and gave me back my pride.
It was not so much your smile that made me glad, But the thought that one day,
You'd be calling me dad.
No longer do I sit and ponder,
If my life is going under.
You make my life worth living,
And you make my life worth giving.
You're daddy's little man, so while you're maturing,
I will work on a future plan.
I will give you my all, and will pick you up whenever you fall.
So when I am old and gray, and can't pick up my footstep, My son, I will look for your help.
Because there is one thing, I can say,
In my heart you will always stay.

ACTIVITY PAGE FOR THE KIDS!

Name:
Date:
Poem Title:

Create your own poem. Use your imagination and be creative!

La Charla con Mi Hijo

El 7 de Agosto de 1997 mi hijo lloró,
Verte venir a este mundo me hizo sentir orgulloso.
Nunca hubo duda o "tal vez",
Yo supe que eras mi bebé.
Cuando te vi sonreír por primera vez,
Estuve tan feliz de que fueras mi niño.
Antes de que vinieras a mi vida, me sentaba y
Reflexionaba sobre cómo la vida te hace preguntarte
Si la vivir vale la pena,
Cuando parece ser que solo has dado,
La mitad de las veces, en mi mente, sentí que perdía,
Porque todo era tan confuso.
Justo cuando había puesto todo de lado,
Viniste y me devolviste el orgullo.
No fue tanto que tu sonrisa me hiciera feliz,
Sino la sensación de que un día,
Me llamarías papá.
Ya no me siento y reflexiono,
Si mi vida si mi vida se hunde.
Haces que mi vida valga la pena.
Y haces que mi vida valga la pena darla.
Eres el pequeño de papá, así que mientras creces,

Trabajaré en un plan a futuro.
Te daré mi todo y te recogeré cuando caigas.
Para cuando sea viejo y gris y no pueda acelerar
el paso, hijo Mío, buscaré tu ayuda.
Porque hay una cosa que puedo decir,
Te quedarás en mi corazón.

¡ Página de Actividades para los Niños!

Nombre:	
Fecha:	
Título del Poema:	

Crea tu propio poema. ¡Usa tu imaginación y sé creativo!

Kids Stay In School

A promise to stay in school is the golden rule,
Because some kids will struggle with school.
Parents should make themselves this promise,
A promise to keep them in school
Is their golden rule.
To always be there for their kids,
To teach them just like their parents did.
Most kids want to do things without their parents,
But a parent should always stay involved.
Parents have to stop it before it starts,
And the welfare of a kid starts with you.
When parents walk through the mall,
They see kids big and small.
It brings a smile to his or her face.
But when the kid talks back to his mother,
The smile leaves your face,
For a kid to bring shame to his mother,
Is a disgrace.
Your mother brought you into this world,
She could have wanted a boy,
But instead she got a girl.
The mother's outlook doesn't change.
You will be treated the same,
The mother just has to change the baby's name.
Kids, everyday should be like its January first,
You don't have to wait 'til the beginning of the year,
To make a New Year's resolution,
To stay in school every day should be the solution.
Parents, there are no guarantees in life
That your kid won't quit school;
Some kids will act as a fool.
But you as a parent,
You have a golden rule,
And that is trying to keep your kid in school.

ACTIVITY PAGE FOR THE KIDS!

Name:	
Date:	
Poem Title:	

Create your own poem. Use your imagination and be creative!

Los Niños se Quedan en la Escuela

La promesa de quedarse en la escuela es la regla de
oro, porque para algunos niños será difícil la
escuela. Los padres deben hacerse esta promesa.
Una promesa de mantenerlos en la Escuela
Es su regla de oro
Siempre estar ahí para sus hijos,
Enseñarles tal como sus propios padres a ellos.
La mayoría de niños quieren hacer cosas sin sus
Padres, pero un padre siempre debe involucrarse.
Los padres deben detenerlo antes que empiece,
Y el bienestar del niño empieza contigo.
Cuando los padres van por el centro comercial,
Ven niños grandes y pequeños.
Esto pone una sonrisa en su rostro.
Pero cuando el niño contesta a su madre,
La sonrisa deja tu cara,
Porque que un niño avergüence a su mamá,
Es una desgracia.
Tu madre te trajo a este mundo,
Pudo haber querido un niño,

Pero en su lugar le tocó una niña.
El punto de vista de la madre no cambia.
Serás tratado igual,
La madre solo tiene que cambiar el nombre del
bebé. Niños, todos los días deben ser como primero
de Enero, no tienes que esperar al inicio del año,
Para hacer un propósito de año nuevo,
Mantenerte en la escuela todos los días debe ser la
solución.
Padres, no hay garantías en la vida
de que tu hijo no deje la escuela;
Algunos niños actuaran como necios.
Pero tú como padre,
Tú tienes la regla de oro,
Y esta es tratar de mantener a tu hijo en la escuela.

¡ Página de Actividades para los Niños!

Nombre:	
Fecha:	
Título del Poema:	

Crea tu propio poema. ¡Usa tu imaginación y sé creativo!

Always Give God The Glory

You have to keep your eyes on the prize,
When there is a job to do,
You should never worry about the size.
The most important thing is that God is with you.
When you give God the glory,
You can be like David and Goliath in history.
David was a little shepherd boy,
Whom God knew had a great love for his sheep,
The kind of love that nothing could destroy.
A bear and a lion one day
Tried to show him his grave,
He killed them both and remained brave.
Goliath was a giant in size,
He took his eyes off the prize.
The Philistines feared him more than God.
When Goliath went against God,
He looked at David and laughed.
He said, "You are so small,
I am Goliath and I am almost ten feet tall."
Goliath said, "My power is in my spear,
You Israelites better never come near."
David said, "My power is in the God of Abraham;
My god is why I am.
When a bear and a lion came looking for a meal,
My God met me in the field."
David took a stone and hit Goliath in the head.
The Israelites rejoiced because the giant had fallen dead.
Whatever you do in life, always put God first
And always give God the glory,
Your life will be a forever-reading story

ACTIVITY PAGE FOR THE KIDS!

Name:	
Date:	
Poem Title:	

Create your own poem. Use your imagination and be creative!

Siempre Dale Gloria a Dios

Debes tener tus ojos en la meta,
Cuando hay un trabajo que hacer,
Nunca deber preocuparte por su tamaño.
Lo más importante es que Dios está contigo.
Cuando das gloria a Dios,
Puedes ser como la historia de David y Goliat.
David era un pequeño pastorcillo,
Que Dios sabía tenía gran amor por sus ovejas,
El tipo de amor que nada puede destruir.
Un oso y un león un día
Trataron de llevarle a su tumba,
Él mató a ambos y se mantuvo valiente.
Goliat era gigante,
Él quitó sus ojos de la meta.
Los Filisteos le temían más a él que a Dios.
Cuando Goliat fue contra Dios,
Vio a David y se rió.
Le dijo,"Eres tan pequeño,
Soy Goliat y tengo casi diez pies de altura."
Goliat dijo, "Mi poder está en mi lanza,

Ustedes los Israelitas mejor ni se acerquen."
David dijo, "Mi poder está en el Dios de Abraham;
Mi Dios es mi razón de ser.
Cuando vinieron el león y el oso buscando su
comida, Mi Dios estuvo conmigo en el campo."
David tomó una piedra y le dio a Goliat en la cabeza.
Los Israelitas se regocijaron porque el gigante había
caído muerto.
Sea lo que sea que hagas en la vida, siempre pon a
Dios primero y siempre dale gloria a Dios,
Tu vida será una de siempre leer.

¡Página de Actividades para los Niños!

Nombre:
Fecha:
Título del Poema:

Crea tu propio poema. ¡Usa tu imaginación y sé creativo!

Who Could It Be?

He won
The World Heavyweight Title in 1964.
He'd done
What no man had done before.
He was champion of the world three times. He gave
The American people so many thrills.
Like the "Thriller from Manila,"
He made
The whole world stand still.
His name was a freedom symbol.
On Olympic day,
He carried the torch,
He kept walking,
As his hand trembled.
He has always had a strong desire;
No one can put out his fire.
He made boxing fun,
And more than just a sport.
He is a true role model,
Whom the world showed a lot of support.
He has been called "The greatest of all time."
He was Sports Illustrated's 20th Century Man.
Think a little harder if you can.
He is a legend in the boxing Hall of Fame.
Cassius Clay is no longer his name.
Who could this gentleman be?
They say he floats like a butterfly,
And stings like a bee.
This man has to be Muhammad Ali.

ACTIVITY PAGE FOR THE KIDS!

Name:
Date:
Poem Title:

Create your own poem. Use your imagination and be creative!

¿Quién Podrá Ser?

Él ganó
El Título de Campeón Pesos Pesados del Mundo en
1964.
Lo que ningún otro hombre había hecho.
Fue campeón del mundo tres veces. Les dio
A los americanos tantas emociones.
Como el "Suspense en Manila,"
Hizo que
Todo el mundo se quedara quieto.
Su nombre fue símbolo de libertad.
En el día Olímpico,
Llevó la antorcha,
Continuó caminando,
Mientras su mano temblaba.
Siempre tuvo un fuerte deseo;
Nadie puede apagar su fuego.
Hizo el boxeo entretenido,
Y más que solo un deporte.
Es un verdadero modelo a seguir,
A quien el mundo mostró mucho apoyo.
Se le ha llamado "El mejor de todos los tiempos."
Fue el Hombre del Siglo 20 de Sports Illustrated

Piensa un poco más si puedes.
Él es una leyenda en el Salón de la Fama del Boxeo.
Su nombre ya no es Casius Clay.
¿Quién puede ser este caballero?
Dicen que flota como mariposa,
Y pica como abeja.
Este hombre tiene que ser Muhammad Alí.

27

¡ Página de Actividades para los Niños!

Nombre:	
Fecha:	
Título del Poema:	

Crea tu propio poema. ¡Usa tu imaginación y sé creativo!

The Lord's Prayer

Our father,
Which art in heaven,
Hollowed Be thy name.
Thy Kingdom Come.
Thy will be done In earth,
As it is in heaven.
Give us this day our daily bread and
Forgive us our debts,
As we forgive our debtors.
And Lead us not
Into temptation, But
Deliver us from evil;
For thine Is the Kingdom,
And the Power,
And the Glory,
Forever.
Amen.

ACTIVITY PAGE FOR THE KIDS!

Name:	
Date:	
Poem Title:	

Create your own poem. Use your imagination and be creative!

La Oración del Señor

Padre nuestro,
Que estás en los cielos,
Santificado sea tu nombre.
Venga a nosotros tu reino.
Hágase tu voluntad en la tierra,
como en el cielo.
Danos hoy nuestro pan de cada día;
Perdona nuestras ofensas,
Como también nosotros perdonamos
a los que nos ofenden.
No nos dejes caer en la tentación
Y líbranos del mal;
Ya que tuyo es el Reino,
Y el Poder,
Y la Gloria,
Por siempre.
Amén.

¡ Página de Actividades para los Niños!

| Nombre: |
| Fecha: |
| Título del Poema: |

Crea tu propio poema. ¡Usa tu imaginación y sé creativo!

Meeting My Son's School Teacher

We had a meeting about my son
She explained to me,
All he had done.
He got off
To a slow start.
He understands,
He must work hard In order to be smart.
His teacher
Went on and on.
She had nothing
But good things to say.
She said
He wants to win,
And that
He has so many friends.
I wish he were there
To see how much
His teacher really cares.
What a thrill,
Hard to say
How I feel.
Can't wait to get home,
To let him know
How proud I am of him.
I know he works hard.
He got a free bowling pass
Because he had a perfect attendance card.

ACTIVITY PAGE FOR THE KIDS!

Name:
Date:
Poem Title:

Create your own poem. Use your imagination and be creative!

Reuniéndome con la Maestra de Mi Hijo

Tuvimos una reunión sobre mi hijo
Me explicó,
Todo lo que había hecho.
Él empezó lento.
Él entiende,
Que debe esforzarse para poder ser listo.
Su maestra,
Continuó.
No tenía sino
Cosas buenas para decir.
Dijo
Que él quiere ganar,
Y que
Tiene tantos amigos.
Me gustaría estar ahí
Para ver lo mucho
Que a su maestra le importa de verdad.
Que emoción,
Es difícil de decir
Como me siento
No puedo esperar a llegar a casa,

Para hacerle saber
Lo orgulloso que estoy de él.
Sé que trabaja duro.
Se ganó un pase de bolos gratis
Porque tiene una lista de asistencia perfecta.

¡ Página de Actividades para los Niños!

Nombre:	
Fecha:	
Título del Poema:	

Crea tu propio poema. ¡Usa tu imaginación y sé creativo!

A Penny On Head

Good luck, Bad luck
How long does it last;
I don't know,
But I have been told,
About
A tale of the past.
The story goes,
If you
Find a penny on head,
Pick it up,
Put it into your pocket,
And
Good luck
Will come your way.
If you
Find a penny on tails,
Pick it up,
And
Throw it away,
But
Bad luck
Will come your way.
If I find
A penny on head,
Good luck
Will come my way.
If I find
A penny on tails,
I'm going to
Flip it over to head,
Put it in my pocket,
So good luck can come my way.

ACTIVITY PAGE FOR THE KIDS!

Name:
Date:
Poem Title:

Create your own poem. Use your imagination and be creative!

Un Centavo de Cara

Buena suerte, Mala suerte
Qué tanto dura;
No lo sé,
Pero me han dicho,
Sobre
Una historia pasada.
La historia dice,
Si tu
Te encuentras un centavo de cara,
Recógelo,
Ponlo en tu bolsillo,
Y
Tendrás
Buena suerte,
Si tu
Te encuentras un centavo de cruz,
Recógelo
Y tíralo,
Pero
Tendrás
Mala suerte

Si me encuentro
Un centavo de cara,
Tendré
Buena Suerte.
Si me encuentro
Un centavo de cruz,
Lo giraré
Para que esté de cara,
Lo pondré en mi bolsillo,
Para tener buena suerte.

¡Página de Actividades para los Niños!

| Nombre: |
| Fecha: |
| Título del Poema: |

Crea tu propio poema. ¡Usa tu imaginación y sé creativo!

Grandparents

They know
Just what to do.
They are the remedy For your kids
And you.
When the kids,
Are under the weather,
They have a way
Of making them feel better.
You sometimes
Have to make that call
When the kids,
Are driving you
Up the wall?
You just
Want a break,
No more can you take.
So you
Load the kids
In the car
And head
To the Grandparents house,
Who don't live far.
Grandparents
Are special and dear,
And
Have a way of letting you know
That they Are always near.

ACTIVITY PAGE FOR THE KIDS!

Name:
Date:
Poem Title:

Create your own poem. Use your imagination and be creative!

Abuelos

Ellos saben
Justamente lo que se debe hacer.
Son el remedio para tus hijos
y para ti.
Cuando los niños,
No se sienten bien,
Tienen una forma
De hacerles sentir mejor.
A veces tú
Tienes que tomar esa decisión
Cuándo los niños
Te tienen estresado
Solo quieres
Un descanso,
Ya no puedes más.
Entonces
Metes a los niños
Al auto
Y vas

Hacia la casa de los Abuelos,

Que no viven lejos.

Los abuelos
Son especiales y queridos,
Y
Tienen una forma de hacerte saber
Que siempre están cerca.

¡Página de Actividades para los Niños!

Nombre:	
Fecha:	
Título del Poema:	

Crea tu propio poema. ¡Usa tu imaginación y sé creativo!

The Barber Shop

Fade
Edge
Hair design
Get it all,
It's your call.
Your input,
The wait can be long While you sit
On your butt.
You will wait,
There is nothing
Like a fresh haircut.
People come
From all round.
You sit and watch
Hair falling down
To the ground.
Kids running
Here and there,
All you
Can do
Is stare.
You are the king
When they call your name.
That sound from the clippers
Is the sweetest thing.
The wait is over
Jump into the chair
And let the barber cut your hair.

ACTIVITY PAGE FOR THE KIDS!

Name:	
Date:	
Poem Title:	

Create your own poem. Use your imagination and be creative!

La Barbería

Peine
Navaja
Estilo de cabello
Háztelo todo,
Es tu decisión.
Tu aporte,
La espera puede ser larga mientras te sientas
En tu trasero.
Esperarás,
No hay nada
Como un corte de cabello fresco.
La gente viene
De todos lados.
Te sientas y ves
El cabello caer
Al suelo.
Niños corriendo
Aquí y allá
Todo lo que puedes
Hacer
Es observar.
Eres el rey
Cuando te llaman.
El sonido de las tijeras
Es lo más dulce.
La espera acabó
Súbete a la silla
Y deja que el barbero te corte el cabello.

¡ Página de Actividades para los Niños!

Nombre:	
Fecha:	
Título del Poema:	

Crea tu propio poema. ¡Usa tu imaginación y sé creativo!

Coffee And Tea

Coffee
Coffee
Tea
Tea
I like coffee,
I like tea,
Which one
Will it be.
May I have a cup,
Just fill it up.
Which one,
Coffee or Tea.
Can't make
My mind up,
Just pour me a cup
Of coffee and tea.
Which one
I drink,
We will have to see.
Is today
Wednesday,
The middle weekday,
The day
We call hump day.
My eyes are in a slump;
Give me
Coffee and tea
To get me over the hump.
Pour me a fresh cup.
Let me
Smell that smell.
If it's flavor
Everyone can tell.
They will finish the pot,
Nothing like Coffee and Tea, hot.

ACTIVITY PAGE FOR THE KIDS!

Name:	
Date:	
Poem Title:	

Create your own poem. Use your imagination and be creative!

Café y Té

Café
Café
Té
Té
Me gusta el café,
Me gusta el té,
¿Cuál de los dos
será?
¿Me das una taza?
Solo llénala.
¿Cuál?
Café o Té.
No me puedo
Decidir,
Solo sírveme una taza
De café y té.
Cuál de los dos
Tomaré,
Tendremos que verlo.
Es hoy,
Miércoles,
El día de mitad de la semana.

El día al que
Llamamos de joroba.
Mis ojos están caídos;
Dame
Café y té
Para pasar la joroba
Sírveme una taza fresca.
Déjame
Oler el aroma.
Si todos pueden
Sentir su sabor.
Se acabarán la olla,
No hay nada como Café y Té, calientes

51

¡ Página de Actividades para los Niños!

Nombre:	
Fecha:	
Título del Poema:	

Crea tu propio poema. ¡Usa tu imaginación y sé creativo!

Born In Alabama

Football
Is the talk.
Eufaula, Alabama is my hometown,
People come from all around.
To fish
And hunt,
They are happy to see
The winter months.
Football
Fishing
Hunting
What more
Could you ask for.
Where these sports
Are bigger than life.
Where you see
The husband,
Usually you see
The wife.
In Alabama,
To have been born,
To pull a cow by the horn,
Is something special for me.
The place
Will always be dear,
Growing up a country boy.
I didn't always speak clear.
But,
All anyone wants to know
Is, who are you for,
Auburn Tigers or Alabama Crimson Tide?

ACTIVITY PAGE FOR THE KIDS!

Name:	
Date:	
Poem Title:	

Create your own poem. Use your imagination and be creative!

Born In Alabama

Del fútbol americano
Es de lo que se habla.
Eufala, Alabama es mi ciudad natal,
La gente viene de todos lados
A pescar
Y cazar,
Se alegran de ver
Los meses de invierno.
Fútbol
Pesca
Caza
¿Qué más se puede pedir?
Donde estos deportes
Son más grandes que la vida.
Donde ves
Al esposo,
Por lo general ves
A la esposa.
En Alabama,
Haber nacido,
El halar a una vaca por los cuernos,

Es algo especial para mí.
El lugar
Siempre será querido,
Al crecer siendo un niño del campo.
No siempre hablaba claro.
Pero,
Todo lo que todos quieren saber
Es ¿Por quién vas,
Los Auburn Tigers o la Alabama
Crimson Tide?

¡Página de Actividades para los Niños!

Nombre:	
Fecha:	
Título del Poema:	

Crea tu propio poema. ¡Usa tu imaginación y sé creativo!

McDonald's

My son's
Favorite place to eat.
It's No problem With getting him To sit in his seat.
Hamburger, Cheeseburger, French fries,
He points
With his eyes.
He Is
Full of joy.
He knows
The happy meal pack
Has a snack
Or a special toy.
When
It's time to go
He runs
To do the door,
And falls on the floor.
The rides he found,
And wants to go on the playground.
As he
Begins to cry
I hand him
A French fry,
A smile
Comes to his face.
A voice speaks;
My name is Ronald,
I'm glad you came to McDonald's.

ACTIVITY PAGE FOR THE KIDS!

Name:	
Date:	
Poem Title:	

Create your own poem. Use your imagination and be creative!

McDonald's

El lugar favorito para comer
De mi hijo.
No hay problema al hacer que se siente en su silla.
Hamburguesa, hamburguesa con queso, papas fritas,
Él las señala
Con sus ojos.
Está
Lleno de alegría.
Él sabe que
El paquete de cajita feliz
Tiene un bocadillo
O un juguete especial.
Cuando es hora de irnos
Él corre
A la puerta,
Y se cae al piso.
Encontró las atracciones,
Y quiere ir al patio de juegos.
Cuando él
Empieza a llorar
Le doy

Una papa frita,
Se dibuja
Una sonrisa en su cara.
Una voz dice;
Mi nombre es Ronald,
Me alegra que vinieras a McDonald's

59

¡Página de Actividades para los Niños!

| Nombre: |
| Fecha: |
| Título del Poema: |

Crea tu propio poema. ¡Usa tu imaginación y sé creativo!

Merry-Go-Round

The Merry-Go-Round
The Merry-Go-Round
The Merry-Go-Round,
It goes
Round and round.
It's like a spinning
top. No one knows
Where it will stop.
Your head
May feel a little light,
But hold on tight.
Drag your feet on the ground.
Who cares
About falling down.
The ride,
Going in circles
And more circles.
You want it to last,
You and your friends
Are having a blast.
Someone hollow more,
So someone push more.
All of a sudden
You hear this thunder,
The gray clouds
Take away the sun,
Just when,
Everyone is having fun.
No more daylight.
The Merry-Go-Round Is
closed for the night.
You and your friends
Had a blast.
You had fun
As long as the ride last.

ACTIVITY PAGE FOR THE KIDS!

Name:
Date:
Poem Title:

Create your own poem. Use your imagination and be creative!

Carrusel

El carrusel
El carrusel
El carrusel,
Da
Vueltas y vueltas.
Es como un trompo
que gira. Nadie sabe
Dónde parará.
Te puedes sentir un poco mareado,
Pero agárrate fuerte.
Arrastra tus pies en el piso.
A quien le importa
Caerse.
La atracción,
Va en círculos
Y más círculos.
Quieres que dure,
Tú y tus amigos
Se divierten un montón.
Alguien húndalo más,
Así que alguien empuje más.

De repente
Escuchas tronar,
Las nubes grises
Se llevan al sol,
Justo cuando
Todos se divierten.
No hay más luz solar.
El carrusel
está cerrado de noche.
Tú y tus amigos
Se divirtieron un montón
Te divertiste
Por lo que duró la atracción.

¡Página de Actividades para los Niños!

| Nombre: |
| Fecha: |
| Título del Poema: |

Crea tu propio poema. ¡Usa tu imaginación y sé creativo!

I Love To Swing

I love to swing
I love to swing
I love to swing,
I don't care
If I get a bang.
I love to swing
I love to swing
I love to swing,
Whatever
My parents ask
To swing,
I'll do anything.
I love
To swing fast.
I love
To swing slow.
I love
To try to touch the sky,
And watch
The birds fly by.
When I swing,
I love to race.
When I swing,
I like to compete,
And win first place.
To swing
How fast,
To swing
How slow,
I don't care,
Just don't let me fall below.

ACTIVITY PAGE FOR THE KIDS!

Name:	
Date:	
Poem Title:	

Create your own poem. Use your imagination and be creative!

Me Encanta Columpiarme

Me encanta columpiarme
Me encanta columpiarme
Me encanta columpiarme,
No me importa
Si me golpeo.
Me encanta columpiarme
Me encanta columpiarme
Me encanta columpiarme,
Lo que sea que
Me pidan mis padres.
Para columpiarme,
Haré cualquier cosa.
Me encanta
Columpiarme rápido
Me encanta
Columpiarme lento
Me encanta
Tratar de tocar el cielo
Y ver
Las aves pasar volando.
Cuando me columpio,
Me encanta hacer carreras

Cuando me columpio,
Me gusta competir,
Y ganar el primer lugar.
Columpiarme
Cuán rápido,
Columpiarme
Cuán lento,
No me importa,
Solo no me dejes caer.

¡ Página de Actividades para los Niños!

Nombre:	
Fecha:	
Título del Poema:	

Crea tu propio poema. ¡Usa tu imaginación y sé creativo!

Putting Your Children To Bed

They fight sleep
Back and forth,
You go into the room to take a peep.
Nothing like a baby's scent,
You take a sniff,
And a kiss on the cheek.
It's a way of speaking,
And hope
They remain sleeping.
Oh well,
Another story to tell,
One opens,
And you take a look,
Time to read another book.
You go
To the rocking chair,
While
They eat, look and stare.
With your mouth closed,
You begin hum and rock,
Staring at the clock.
It's going to be
A long night,
You can't even dim the light.
A hush comes
When you hear noise,
Everything must be quiet;
A sudden sound
Can take away the poise.
Silence and stillness,
So you rub their head
And slowly put them into bed.
You go to your room
Knowing you have to wake up soon.

ACTIVITY PAGE FOR THE KIDS!

Name:	
Date:	
Poem Title:	

Create your own poem. Use your imagination and be creative!

Acostando a Tus Hijos

Se resisten al sueño
Un forcejeo,
Vas al cuarto a echar un vistazo.
No hay nada como el aroma de un bebé,
Lo olfateas,
Y le das un beso en la mejilla.
Es una forma de hablar,
Y esperas
Que sigan durmiendo.
Bueno,
Otra historia para contar,
Uno se abre,
Y echas un vistazo,
Es hora de leer otro libro.
Vas
A la mecedora,
Mientras
Ellos comen y observan.
Con tu boca cerrada
Empiezas a tararear y a mecerte,
Observando el reloj.
Será

Una noche larga,
Ni siquiera puedes bajar la luz. Llega
un silencio
Cuando escuchas ruido,
Todo debe estar callado;
Un sonido repentino
Puede quitar el equilibrio.
El silencio y la quietud,
Así que acaricias su cabeza.
Y lentamente los acuestas.
Vas a tu cuarto
Sabiendo que debes levantarte pronto

¡ Página de Actividades para los Niños!

Nombre:
Fecha:
Título del Poema:

Crea tu propio poema. ¡Usa tu imaginación y sé creativo!

Time-Out

Kids
Don't always do
What mommy or daddy say,
Time-out,
A place
They have to go.
Good behavior
Can shorten
The time they stay.
Bad behavior
Can make
It a long day.
They have
To understand
The correct way.
As a child
They must be trained early,
So they don't run wild.
This is our task,
Help from someone else,
We shouldn't have to ask.
It hurts us
As parents.
It's like having a list
Of what to do,
And how much did we miss.
We don't
Want to move anything
To the next day,
We call time out,
And get it out of the way.

ACTIVITY PAGE FOR THE KIDS!

Name:
Date:
Poem Title:

Create your own poem. Use your imagination and be creative!

Tiempo Fuera

Los niños
No siempre hacen
Lo que papá o mamá dicen,
Tiempo fuera,
Un espacio
Al que tienen que ir.
El buen comportamiento
Puede acortar
El tiempo que dura.
El mal comportamiento
Puede volverlo
Un día largo.
Tienen que
Entender
Lo que es correcto.
Como niños
Deben ser instruidos temprano,
Para que no se vuelvan locos.
Esta es nuestra tarea,
Ayudar a alguien más,
No deberíamos pedirlo.
Nos hiere

Como padres.
Es como tener una lista
de qué hacer,
Y de cuanto nos faltó.
No queremos dejar nada
Para el día siguiente,
Pedimos tiempo fuera,
Y nos ocupamos de eso.

¡ Página de Actividades para los Niños!

Nombre:	
Fecha:	
Título del Poema:	

Crea tu propio poema. ¡Usa tu imaginación y sé creativo!

The Rain Song

Little Brandon wants to play
Little Brandon wants to play
Little Brandon wants to play
Little Brandon wants to play,
But The sun is not shinning today.
Sing.
I wish it wouldn't rain
I wish it wouldn't rain
I wish it wouldn't rain
I wish it wouldn't rain,
Why does water
Fall on the window pane.
Sing,
The sun is not shinning today
The sun is not shinning today
The sun is not shinning today
The sun is not shinning today,
Little Brandon wants to play.
I wish it wouldn't rain
I wish it wouldn't rain
I wish it wouldn't rain
I wish it wouldn't rain
Little Brandon
He wants to play,
Please rain go away
Please rain go away
Please rain go away,
And come again another day.

ACTIVITY PAGE FOR THE KIDS!

Name:	
Date:	
Poem Title:	

Create your own poem. Use your imagination and be creative!

La Canción de la Lluvia

El pequeño Brandon quiere jugar
El pequeño Brandon quiere jugar
El pequeño Brandon quiere jugar
El pequeño Brandon quiere jugar,
Pero el sol no brilla hoy.
Canta.
Ojalá no lloviera
Ojalá no lloviera
Ojalá no lloviera
Ojalá no lloviera,
¿Por qué cae el agua
a la ventana?
Canta,
El sol no brilla hoy
El sol no brilla hoy
El sol no brilla hoy
El sol no brilla hoy
El pequeño Brandon quiere jugar
Ojalá no lloviera
Ojalá no lloviera
Ojalá no lloviera
Ojalá no lloviera

El pequeño Brandon
quiere jugar,
Por favor vete lluvia
Por favor vete lluvia
Por favor vete lluvia,
Y regresa otro día.

¡ Página de Actividades para los Niños!

Nombre:	
Fecha:	
Título del Poema:	

Crea tu propio poema. ¡Usa tu imaginación y sé creativo!

Giraffe

Boys and Girls,
Did you know
The Giraffe,
Is the tallest
Animal in the world?
Boys and Girls,
Did you know,
In the jungle
They are easily found,
Its head
Is high above the ground.
The Giraffe
Can see
A very long distance,
If danger is near,
It can move instantly.
They have long legs
And run very fast.
With their speed,
Most animals they will pass.
The Giraffe
Loves to eat leaves;
It has one advantage,
It can reach high
And get leaves from the trees.
Boys and Girls,
Now you know
The Giraffe
Is the tallest
Animal in the world.

ACTIVITY PAGE FOR THE KIDS!

Name:	
Date:	
Poem Title:	

Create your own poem. Use your imagination and be creative!

Jirafa

Niños y Niñas,
¿Sabían que
La Jirafa
Es el animal más alto
En el mundo?
Niños y Niñas
¿Sabían que
En la jungla
Se les encuentra fácilmente?
Su cabeza
Está alta sobre el suelo.
La Jirafa
Puede ver
Muy lejos,
Si hay peligro cerca,
Se puede mover inmediatamente.
Tienen piernas largas
Y corren muy rápido.
Con su velocidad,
Pasan a la mayoría de animales.
A la Jirafa
Le encanta comer hojas;

Tiene la ventaja
De alcanzar alto
Y coger las hojas de los árboles.
Niños y Niñas,
Ahora saben
Que la Jirafa
Es el animal
Más alto en el mundo.

¡ Página de Actividades para los Niños!

| Nombre: |
| Fecha: |
| Título del Poema: |

Crea tu propio poema. ¡Usa tu imaginación y sé creativo!

The Chimpanzee

Boys and Girls,
Did you know
The Chimpanzee,
Is one
Of the smartest animals in the world.
Boys and Girls,
Did you know
Like humans,
They can get diseases,
Such as tuberculosis
And cancer.
A chimpanzee,
Can been taught
To say some words.
They have been able to,
In some cases
Give the right answer.
Like humans
They can walk on two feet.
Boys and Girls,
Did you know
The chimpanzee,
Has been compared to man.
They can do
What most humans can do.
They have learned
To do sign language.
The chimpanzee,
Is one
Of the smartest animals
In the world.

ACTIVITY PAGE FOR THE KIDS!

Name:	
Date:	
Poem Title:	

Create your own poem. Use your imagination and be creative!

El Chimpancé

Niños y Niñas,
¿Sabían que
El Chimpancé
Es uno de los animales más listos en el mundo?
Niños y Niñas,
¿Sabían que
Tal como a los humanos
Les pueden dar enfermedades,
Tales como la tuberculosis
y el cáncer?
Se puede enseñar
A un Chimpancé
A decir algunas palabras.
Han sido capaces de,
En ciertos casos,
Dar la respuesta correcta.
Tal como los humanos
Pueden caminar en dos pies.
Niños y Niñas
¿Sabían que
El Chimpancé

Ha sido comparado con los hombres?
Pueden hacer
Lo que la mayoría de humanos pueden.
Han aprendido
El lenguaje de señas.
El chimpancé
Es uno
De los animales más listos
En el mundo.

¡ Página de Actividades para los Niños!

Nombre:
Fecha:
Título del Poema:

Crea tu propio poema. ¡Usa tu imaginación y sé creativo!

The Turtle

Boy and Girls,
Did you know
The leatherback,
Is the largest turtle In the world.
They are so big,
That a small child
Could ride on its back.
Boys and Girls,
Did you know
They can swim fast.
The leatherback,
You can't
Hold in your hand,
Sometimes,
It comes on land.
It weighs about 600 pounds.
The sea,
Is where it can be found.
Boys and Girls,
Really,
Did you know The leatherback
Is the largest turtle In the
world.

ACTIVITY PAGE FOR THE KIDS!

Name:	
Date:	
Poem Title:	

Create your own poem. Use your imagination and be creative!

La Tortuga

Niños y Niñas,
¿Sabían que
La tortuga laúd
Es la tortuga más grande en el mundo?
Son tan grandes,
Que un niño pequeño
Podría montarse en su lomo.
Niños y Niñas,
¿Sabían que
Pueden nadar rápido?
A la tortuga laúd,
No la puedes coger con la mano,
A veces,
Va a tierra.
Pesa como 600 libras.
El mar,
Es donde se le puede encontrar.

Niños y Niñas,
En serio,
¿Sabían que la tortuga laúd
es la tortuga más grande
en el mundo?

¡ Página de Actividades para los Niños!

Nombre:	
Fecha:	
Título del Poema:	

Crea tu propio poema. ¡Usa tu imaginación y sé creativo!

Komodo Dragons

Boys and Girls,
Did you know
Komodo dragons
Are the largest lizards,
In the world?
There is an old saying
That they can breathe fire.
They can't breathe fire, You don't
Have to stay inside,
But you must beware.
They don't have wings,
They don't have tails
That'll give you a sting.
Everyone has to watch out!
They are big animals,
When hungry,
They can eat a lot.
They don't change color,
But some lizards can.
They can weigh 300 pounds,
They can grow to be long,
And their teeth are strong.
Boys and Girls,
Did you know
Komodo dragons are the largest lizards
In the world.

ACTIVITY PAGE FOR THE KIDS!

Name:	
Date:	
Poem Title:	

Create your own poem. Use your imagination and be creative!

Dragones de Komodo

Niños y Niñas,
¿Sabían que
Los dragones de komodo
son los lagartos más grandes
en el mundo?
Hay un viejo rumor
De que pueden escupir fuego.
Ellos no escupen fuego, no tienes
Que quedarte adentro,
Pero debes tener cuidado.
No tienen alas,
No tienen colas
Con las que te pican.
¡Todos tienen que tener cuidado!
Son animales grandes,
Cuando tienen hambre
Pueden comer un montón.
No cambian de color,
Pero algunos lagartos si pueden.
Pueden pesar 300 libras,
Pueden ser largos

Y sus dientes son fuertes.
Niños y Niñas,
¿Sabían que
Los dragones de komodo son
Los lagartos más grandes en el mundo?

¡ Página de Actividades para los Niños!

Nombre:
Fecha:
Título del Poema:

Crea tu propio poema. ¡Usa tu imaginación y sé creativo!

Hummingbird

Boys and Girls,
Did you know
The Hummingbird
Is the smallest bird
In the world.
High up on the peak,
Like the hawk and eagle,
You can see
Its little beak.
In the bird's nest,
The eggs
Are not like the rest.
It lays
The smallest eggs.
The Ostrich
Is the biggest bird?
It lays
The biggest eggs.
A hummingbird
Can stand
Still in the air,
As if it's not there.
It can flap
Its wings so fast,
As if it's not moving.
A hummingbird,
Drinks nectar from flowers.
A source of food power.

ACTIVITY PAGE FOR THE KIDS!

Name:
Date:
Poem Title:

Create your own poem. Use your imagination and be creative!

Colibrí

Niños y Niñas,
¿Sabían que
El Colibrí
Es el ave más pequeña
En el mundo?
Arriba en los picos,
Como el halcón y el águila,
Puedes ver
Su pequeño pico.
En el nido del ave,
Los huevos
No son como el resto.
Pone
Los huevos más pequeños.
¿El avestruz
Es el ave más grande?
Pone
Los huevos más grandes.
Un colibrí
Puede permanecer Quieto
en el aire,

Como si no estuviera ahí.
Puede batir
Sus alas tan rápido,
Como si no se moviera.
Un colibrí,
Bebe el néctar de las flores
Una fuente de energía de alimento.

¡ Página de Actividades para los Niños!

Nombre:	
Fecha:	
Título del Poema:	

Crea tu propio poema. ¡Usa tu imaginación y sé creativo!

22 Inspiring Quotes for your Kids

1. "Once you learn to read, you will be forever free." **–Fredrick Douglass**, He was an American social reformer, abolitionist, statesman, and writer. Place of Birth: **Cordova, MD**

2. "I knew that whatever I set my mind to do. I could do."**–Wilma Rudolph**, The first American woman to with three gold medals in track and field at a single Olympics. Place of Birth: **Bethlehem, Tennessee**

3. "Education is the most powerful weapon which you can use to change the world. **–Nelson Mandela**, He was a South African political leader and philanthropist who served as President of South Africa from 1994 to 1999. Place of Birth: **Mvezo, Cape Province, South Africa**

4. "Change will not come if we wait for some other person or some other time. We are the ones we've been waiting for. We are the change that we seek.**–Barack Obama**, The first African American president in the United States of America. Place of Birth: **Honolulu, Hi**

5. "Thank you is the best prayer that anyone could say. I say that one a lot. Thank you expresses extreme gratitude, humility, and understanding." **–Alice Walker**, author of the book The Color Purple. Place of Birth: **Eatonton, Georgia**

6. "Be anything you want to be, but don't be dull."**–Frank Robinson**, The first African American manager in the majors for the Cleveland Indians in 1974. In 1982, he was inducted into the Baseball Hall of Fame. Place of Birth: **Beaumont, Texas.**

7. "I believe there is only one race-the human race."- **Rosa Parks**, The United States Congress has called her "the first lady of civil rights" and "the mother of the freedom movement." Place of Birth: **Tuskegee, AL**

8. "I hated every minute of training, but I said, don't quit. Suffer now and live the rest of your life as a champion." **–Muhammad Ali**, He won the heavyweight title a record-setting three times. Place of Birth: **Louisville, KY**

9. "Life's most persistent and urgent question is, what are you doing for others?"-**Martin Luther King Jr.** He was an American Baptist minister and activist who became the most visible spokesperson and leader in the civil rights movement. Place of Birth: **Atlanta, Georgia**

10. "Life is like a tennis game. You can't win without serving." **–Arthur Ashe**, He was the first black player selected to the United States Davis Cup team and the only black man ever to win the singles title at Wimbledon, the US Open, and the Australian Open. Place of Birth: **Richmond, Virginia**

11. I've learned that people will forget what you said, people will forget what you did, but people will never forget how you made them feel". **–Maya Angelou**, She was an American poet, singer, and worked with Martin Luther King Jr. and Malcolm X in the Civil Rights movement. Place of Birth : **St. Louis, Missouri**

12. "I want to be what I've wanted to be: "Dominant." – **Tiger Woods**, He became the youngest man and the first African American to win the U.S. Masters. Place of Birth: **Cypress, California**

13. –"I truly feel blessed and honored to have that title. I'm excited that my grandkids will be reading about me in history books. -**Vonetta Flowers**, She became the First black person to win a gold medal at the Olympic Winter Games for bobsledder. Vonetta Flowers was inducted in the Alabama Sports Hall of Fame. Place of Birth: **Birmingham, Alabama**

14. "There are better starters than me but I'm a strong finisher." –**Jackie Joyner –Kersee**, The first American woman to win an Olympic gold medal in the long jump. She was named Sports Illustrated for Women's top female athlete of the 20th century. Place of birth: **East St. Louis, Illinois.**

15. "If I had to choose between baseball's Hall of Fame and first class citizenship for all my people. I would say first-class citizenship. " –**Jackie Robinson**, The first African American to play in Major League Baseball. He was inducted into the Baseball Hall of Fame in 1962. Place of Birth: **Cairo, Georgia**

16. "My mother introduced me to many different things, and figure skating was one of them. I just thought that it was magical having to glide across the ice." –**Debra Janine Thomas**, The first African American to win the women's title at the U.S. Figure Skating Championships in 1988. Place of Birth: **Poughkeepie, New York**

17. "Just because a man lacks the use of his eyes doesn't mean he lacks vision." –**Stevie Wonder**, He is considered one of the most successful musical performers. His mother Lula Mae Hardaway was born in Eufaula, Alabama which is my birth place too. Place of Birth for Stevie: **Saginaw, Michigan**

18. "I think I've already got the main thing I've always wanted, which is to be somebody, to have an identify. I'm Althea Gibson, the tennis champion. I hope it makes me happy." –**Althea Gibson**, The first African-American tennis player to compete at the U.S. National Championships in 1950, and the first black player to compete at Wimbledon in 1951. She also broke racial barriers in professional golf. Place of Birth: **Clarendon County, South Carolina**

19. ""Never give up and always keep fighting, because though times may be tough, the sacrifices do pay off, so just keep pushing towards your dream and just love it at the same time and enjoy it."–**Gabby Douglas**, The First African American to win the individual all-around event. She also won gold medals for the U.S. in the team completions at the 2012 and 2016 Olympics. Place of birth: **Newport News, Virginia**

20. "Create the highest, grandest vision possible for your life, because you become what you believe." –Oprah Winfrey, She was awarded the Presidential Medal of Freedom by President Obama. It is the highest civilian award of the United States. It was established in 1963 by John F. Kennedy. Place of Birth: **Kosciusko, Mississippi**

21. "You may not always have a comfortable life and you will not always be able to solve all of the world's problems at once but don't ever underestimate the importance you can have because history has shown us that courage can be contagious and hope can take on a life of its own." –Michelle Obama, Former First Lady of the United States and she was the first African American First Lady. Place of Birth: **Chicago, Illinois**

22. "I want to be an inspiration, but I would like there to be a day when it is not "Simone the black swimmer."–**Simone Manuel**, The First African American swimmer to win an individual Olympic gold medal with her record-setting performance at the 2016 Rio Games. Place of Birth: **Sugar Land, Texas**

About the book

Children's books are fascinating and leave us
with great memories. The most important
things in life are not what you can see, but what
you can read and forever feel in your heart.

Sobre el Libro

Los libros para niños son fascinantes y nos
dejan grandes recuerdos. Las cosas más
importantes de la vida no son las que puedes
ver, sino las que puedes leer y sentir siempre en
tu corazón.

CPSIA information can be obtained
at www.ICGtesting.com
Printed in the USA
BVHW022243280419
546793BV00012B/324/P